PLAY WITH MY BOOBS!

A Titstacular Activity Book for Adults

By D.D. Stacks

Illustrated by Billy Armstrong
and Chessie Wiking

Layout & Design Elements by Dan Nolte

Play With My Boobs
A Titstacular Activity Book for Adults

Images and text © Happy Hen Books

Published by Happy Hen Books
15608 S. New Century Drive
Gardena, CA 90248
www.scbdistributors.com

ISBN: 0-937609-69-9
ISBN-13: 978-0-937609-69-9

First Happy Hen Edition 2014
Second Printing
2 4 6 8 10 9 7 5 3 1

ALSO AVAILABLE

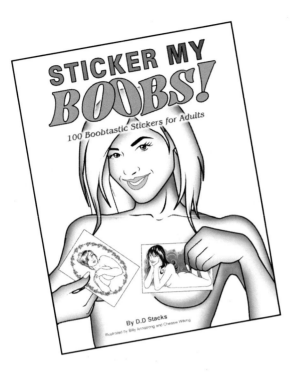

— Visual Answer key —

You'll find the answers to quizzes, matching games and other games
on the game pages ~ upside down and in very small type!

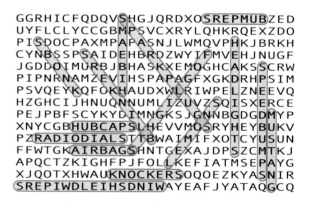

What's the

There are 10 differences between the pictures on the left and right.

1 _____

2 _____

3 _____

4 _____

5 _____

Difference?

Can you find them all?

6 _____

7 _____

8 _____

9 _____

10 _____

Bra on floor; blush on cheeks; lipstick; nipple ring; belt; ankle bracelet; colored nails; watch; buttons on sofa; colored shoes

CONNECT-THE-DOTS

START

END

Treasure Chest

TAKE A TWIRL WITH THE WORDFINDER

Can you find these boob-o-centric words in the grid below?

BABALOOS
BALLOONS
BONGO
BOOB
BOSOM
BREAST
BREASTICLE
BUD
BULBS
CAN

GIRLS
ICBM
JUGS
JUMBO
PACIFIER
PEAKS
TETON
TIT

TITI
TITTY
TWINS

```
O Y A O E C F F G N F D Y F E
Z W S W N N A E O B M U J X I Q
Y B E E D B N M O S O B H L A R O
N O T R J P A C I F I E R Y K F O N
N C X I I S T K R H A O B A X T S R
B E L C I T S A E R B J J K O X G A H N
W D S Y D B A T T W I N S F G P U O I Y Z
G E F L K Z K E U M Y I X E N N D J R J K O T
D I X Q K Z D R T L S H B F M O B X B U L B S L E
I H W S R T V S P B V T L U W S Q B O Z J J E D U D C F
J R K T B L N V C P E T R C Z M L O C L G Q T I T E T O N
J G Z C Q I S O O L A B A B E B O O B I L V P F C H X C K K
B U D S N D T B E L F Z H K I Z B D H X A N H B B A P K U D
T E P A T X S F I J Q I N G R S U R Z E D B H W Y K H W M B O
```

Matching Game

Only two of these six silhouettes are the same.
Can you pick which ones match?

OWN CAPTIONS!

What's the astronaut thinking? What's the alien saying?

International Boob Quiz

Every country has a special word for boobs! Match the country in Column A
with its word for boobs, bosoms or bazooms in Column B.

1. Hawaiian	A. borsten
2. Spanish	B. möpsie
3. Russian	C. mamella
4. Hindi	D. mimi
5. German	E. ü
6. Swahili	F. sis'ki
7. Italian	G. stana
8. Dutch	H. matiti
9. Chinese	I. vyzia
10. Greek	J. teta

BOOBS ON FILM

Match the movie quote in the left column...

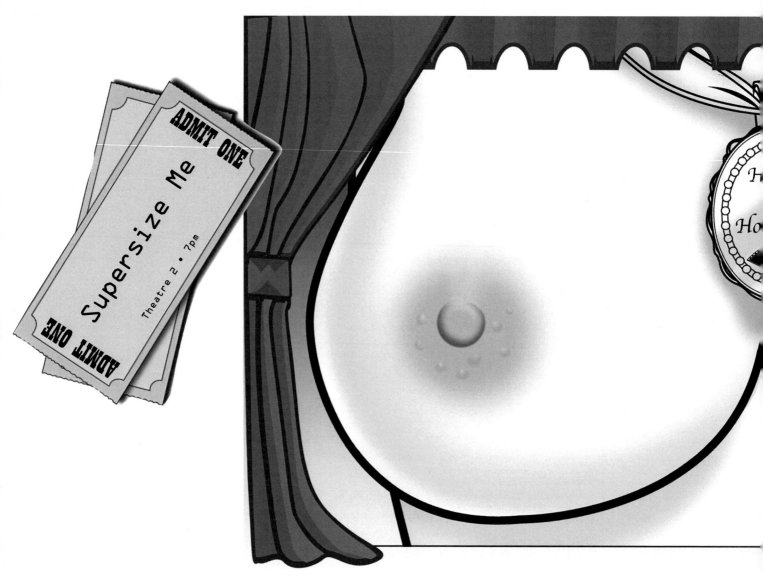

ADMIT ONE

Supersize Me

Theatre 2 • 7pm

ADMIT ONE

QUOTES FROM FILMS

① *"...bodacious tatas..."*

② *"Tits. Hoo-ah! Big ones, little ones, nipples staring right out at ya, like secret searchlights.*

③ *"What Knockers!"*

④ *"Tits McGee!"*

⑤ *"What is it with this girl? She got beer-flavoured nipples?"*

⑥ *"Oh baby, you make me wish I had three hands!"*

⑦ *"I mean your boobs are huge. I mean I want to squeeze them."*

⑧ *"You know how when you grab a woman's breast... it feels like... a bag of sand?"*

⑨ *"She isn't a boy, look at her boobies!"*

MATCHING GAME

...with the film listed in the right column.

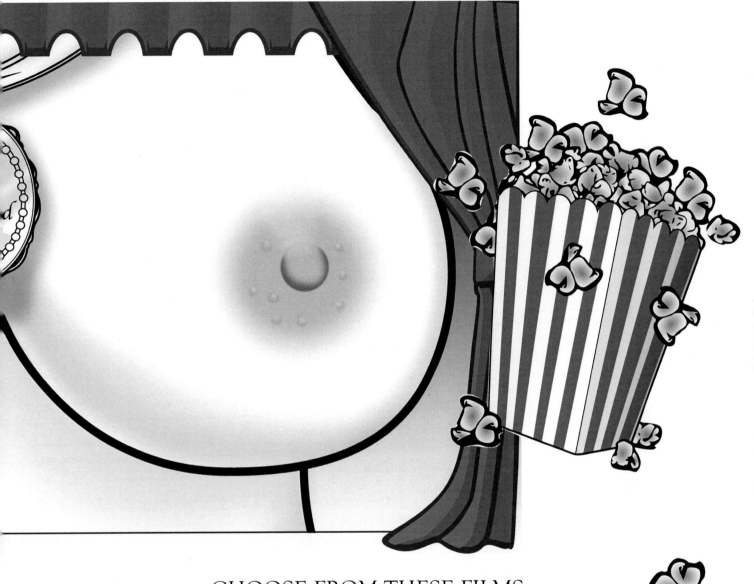

CHOOSE FROM THESE FILMS

(A) An Officer and a Gentleman

(B) Shakespeare in Love

(C) 10 Things I Hate About You

(D) Liar Liar

(E) Scent of a Woman

(F) The 40-Year Old Virgin

(G) Total Recall

(H) Young Frankenstein

(I) Anchorman

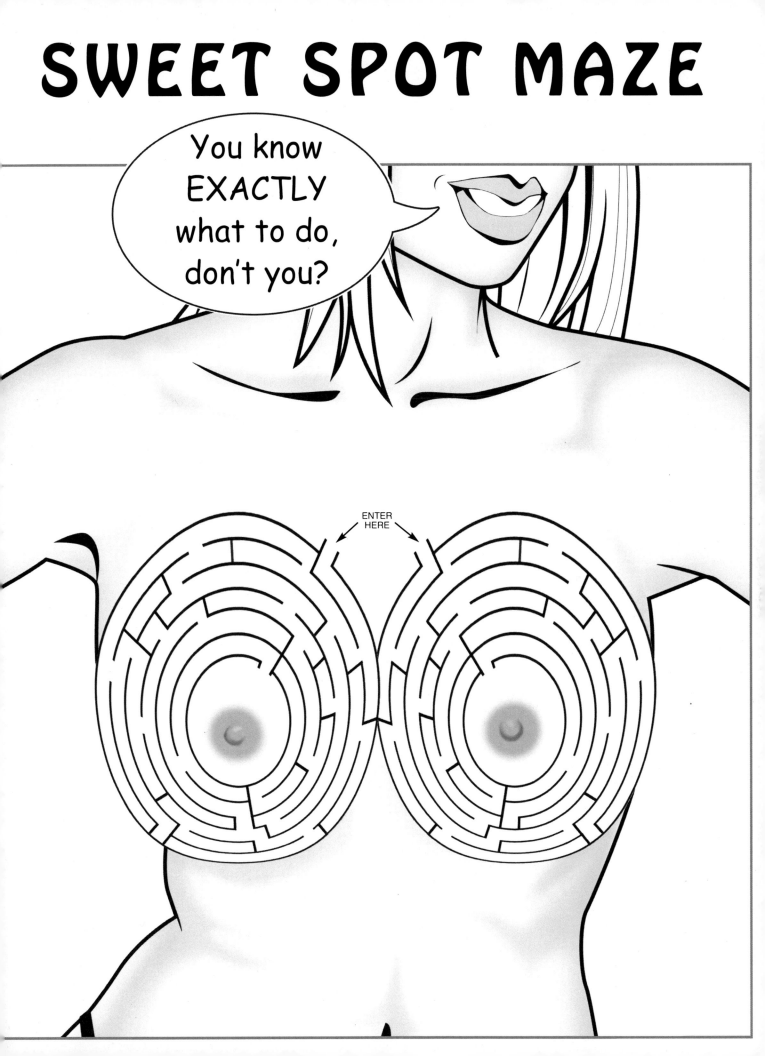

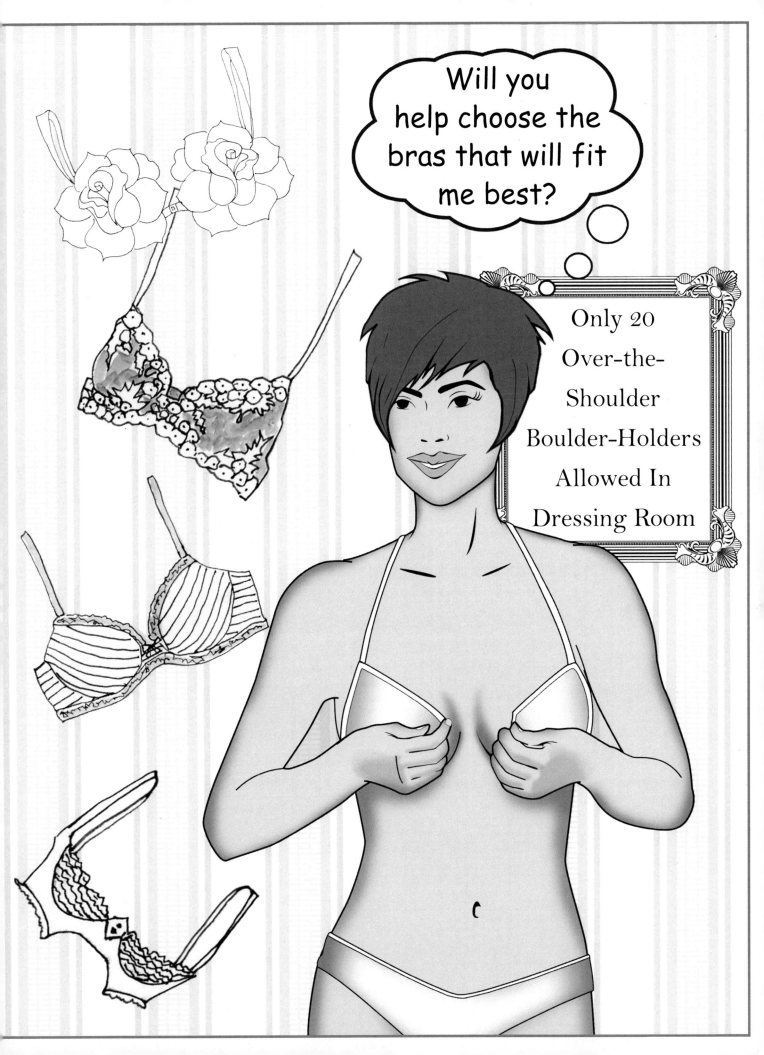

CLASSIC CAR WORDFINDER

Ever notice how many automotive terms refer to boobs?
Can you find these words in the grid below?

WINDSHIELD WIPERS
SPEED BUMPS
RADIO DIALS
LEMONS
KNOBS
KNOCKERS
MUSTANG
BUMPERS
AIRBAGS
SPARK PLUGS
HEADLIGHTS
FOG LIGHTS
HI-BEAMS
HUBCAPS
BLINKERS

G G R H I C F Q D Q V S H G J J Q R D X O S R E P M U B Z E D
U Y F L C L Y C C G B M P S V C X R Y L Q H K R Q E X Z D O
P I S D O C P A X M P A P A S N J L W M Q V P H K J B R K H
C Y N B S S P S A I D E H B R D Z W Y I F M V E H J N U G F
J G D D O I M U R B J B H A S K X E M O G H C A K S S C R W
P I P N R N A M Z E V I H S P A P A G F X G K D R H P S I M
P S V Q E Y K Q F O K H A U D X W L R I W P E L Z N E E V Q
H Z G H C I J H N U Q N N U M L I Z U V Z S Q I S X E R C E
P E J P B F S C Y K Y D I M N G K S J G N N B G D G D M Y P
X N Y C G B H U B C A P S L H E V V M O S R Y H E Y B U K V
P Z R A D I O D I A L S T T B W A I M I F X O T C Y U S U N
F F W T G K A I R B A G S H N T G E X A J D P S Z C M T K J
A P Q C T Z K I G H F P J F O L L K E F I A T M S E P A Y G
X J Q O T X H W A U K N O C K E R S O Q O E Z K Y A S N I R
S R E P I W D L E I H S D N I W A Y E A F J Y A T A Q G C Q

MATCH THE FOOD BOOBS!

Boobs ARE delicious! Draw a line connecting each
word in the middle to its corresponding image.

ICE CREAM CONES

DUMPLINGS

CREAM PUFFS

CUPCAKES

LOLLIPOPS

FRIED EGGS

FLAPJACKS

JUGS

CANS

GUMDROPS

BOOBY AND THE BEAST

A search & replace story – use your imagination to fill in the missing words
to create a one-of-a-kind fantasy tale about a gorgeous princess with the perfect pair...

In an ancient kingdom, the beautiful princess (_____), who
NAME

had the most perfect set of (_____), was exiled to a lonely
NAME FOR BOOBS

(_____) in a (_____) forest by a wizard, in
TYPE OF BUILDING   DESCRIPTIVE ADJECTIVE

order to protect her perfect (_____). She was lonely in her prison,
NAME FOR BOOBS

and spent her time playing (_____) and (_____).
TYPE OF GAME   TYPE OF GAME

One happy day she befriended a (_____) (_____)
DESCRIPTIVE ADJECTIVE   ANIMAL

which (_____) into her lonely home. She tucked her new animal friend
ACTION

between her (_____), fed it, and sang (_____) to it.
NAME FOR BOOBS   NAME OF SONG

So (_____) was the princess for a companion that she (_____)
A FEELING   ACTION VERB

her new animal friend on its (_____)! Magically, it turned into a
BODY PART

(_____) (_____) who looked deep into her
DESCRIPTIVE ADJECTIVE   TYPE OF PERSON

(_____) and said the three words she was longing to hear:
BODY PART

_____ _____ _____.

With these words they became free and lived happily ever after, because

of her (_____) (_____).
DESCRIPTIVE ADJECTIVE   NAME FOR BOOBS

The End

FILL-IN-THE-BLANKS

Why did an Egyptian Queen travel to the New World? Who are those luscious maidens lolling in the lake? Why are there so many birds?

A BLUE-F__TED _____Y WATCHES QUEEN WHILE HER ___TERING, ___TILATING AND A YELLOW-_____ED ___MOUSE. IS THE _____ (extra credit

IN THIS EXOTIC FANTASY

Find out the answers to these questions and more by filling in the missing letters of the story below. There's a bonus if you can read hieroglyphics!!!!

12,507 feet

PERU →
← BOLIVIA

NEFER_ _ _ _ _ FLOAT ON LAKE _ _ _ _ _CACA
HANDMAIDENS OFFER HER A _ _ _ _WILLOW
THE NAME OF QUEEN NEFER_ _ _ _'S BOAT
because it's spelled in hieroglyphics).

THE PLAY WITH MY BOOBS SONG!

Transcribed for Guitar by Phil McCannz

Here are original lyrics to a very familiar tune, the opening bars to Beethoven's 5th Symphony –
you know, the one that starts like this: TA TA TA DUM!

SLEEPY SCRAMBLE

Sweet Sarah wants you to know what's on her mind this morning,
so unscramble the words – and the word order – in these 2 sentences:

1. i'ts oto ot og ot owrk ayrel

___ ___ _____ __ __ __ _____!

2. yhneo reraht tiwh elpse ni yuo dI'

__ _____ _____ __ ____ ___, _____!

CLASSICAL

Boobs have fascinated humans from the beginning of time, and these bounteous beauties were created for your enjoyment by enthralled artists of every era.

SCULPTURES

⑤

①

A. Henry Moore's mommy was a stone cold bench

B. Don't be so sad! Disney made a movie out of you! You're rich!

C. Of course the Sphinx has a girlfriend!

④

D. The hipster hat is cute, but maybe you'd better cut back on the mammoth burgers, Venus

E. You've really got to hand it to her, she's been around a long time

②

③

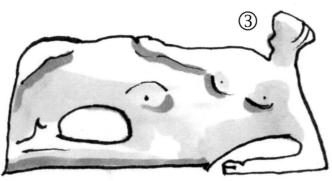

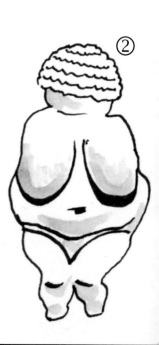

BOOBS

Every piece of art tells a story, so peruse the bosomy babes on each page and then draw a line from the description in the middle of the page to the matching image on that page.

PAINTINGS

⑤

①

A. Hey Modigliani – Why the long face?

B. Picasso was ON something, wasn't he?!

C. ...and an order of steamed clams, Botticelli!

④

D. Nice slippers, Manet!

②

E. Be a postman in France or a beach bum in Tahiti? Gaugin was nobody's fool!

③

BOOBIE TRIVIA QUIZ

1. The English word *breast* derives from:

    A. the Indo-European word for swelling
    B. the Anglo Saxon word for softness
    C. the Native American word for happiness
    D. the French word for playing
    E. the German word for large

2. The shape of classic Champagne glasses imitates whose breasts?

    A. Marilyn Monroe
    B. Venus de Milo
    C. Marie Antoinette
    D. Janet Jackson
    E. Florence Nightingale

3. What does the ancient Indian erotic book, *The Kama Sutra,* recommend regarding breasts?

    A. scratching and biting the breasts
    B. holding each breast tightly
    C. tickling the breasts
    D. licking the breasts
    E. petting the breasts

4. There are many mountains named after breasts, but which of these is completely made up?

    A. the Maiden Paps in Scotland
    B. the Maiden's Breast Mountains in the Philippines
    C. the Bobbling Boobies in Killarney, Ireland
    D. the Breasts of Aphrodite in Mykonos, Greece
    E. the Grand Tetons Range in Wyoming, USA

5. What % of women have breasts of two different sizes?

    A. 20%
    B. 33%
    C. 50%
    D. 75%
    E. 90%

6. The average breast weighs

    A. six ounces
    B. one pound
    C. two pounds
    D. 1/2 pound
    E. one and a half pounds

7. Which of the following is NOT a name for a bra:

    A. Bullet bra
    B. Train Zone bra
    C. Wonder bra
    D. Minimizer bra
    E. Jog bra

8. The areola is located where?

    A.
    B.
    C.
    D.
    E.

What's the Difference?

There are 10 differences between the left and right pictures. Can you find them?

1 _____
2 _____
3 _____
4 _____
5 _____
6 _____
7 _____
8 _____
9 _____
10 _____

lipstick; nose stud; hair coloring; nail polish; chin dimple; ribbon loop end; shadow in ribbon loop; word on ring; additional ring on other hand; missing loop of hair

GET TO KNOW
THIS LINGERIE MODEL

Get intimate with this sultry lingerie model by creating a biography for her.

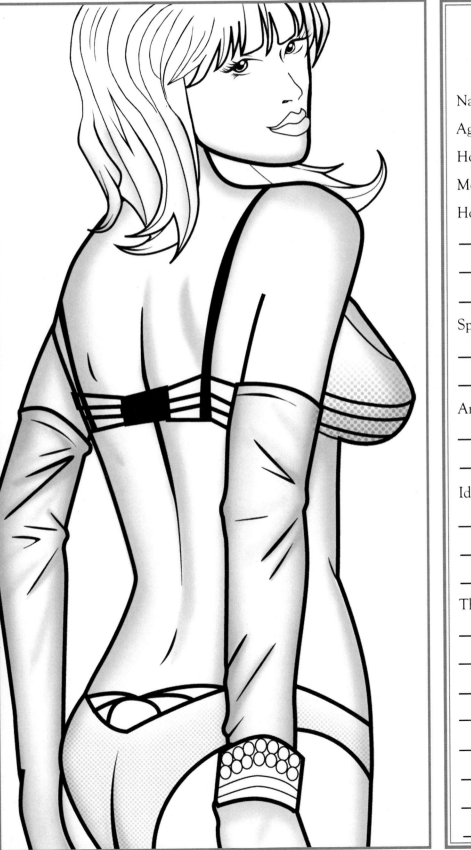

LINGERIE MODEL BIOGRAPHY

Name _____

Age _____

Hometown _____

Measurements _____

Hobbies _____

_____

_____

_____

Special Talent _____

_____

_____

Ambition _____

_____

_____

Ideal Date _____

_____

_____

_____

Thoughts on World Peace _____

_____

_____

_____

_____

_____

_____